Kevin D. Thompson | Mark E. Huglen | Megan N. Bell | Lynnette M. Mullins

PUBLIC SPEAKING
Workbook

Kendall Hunt
publishing company

Cover image © Shutterstock, Inc. Used under license.

Kendall Hunt
publishing company

www.kendallhunt.com
Send all inquiries to:
4050 Westmark Drive
Dubuque, IA 52004-1840

TABLE OF CONTENTS

EXPANDED TABLE OF CONTENTS

PREFACE

This workbook is divided into sections by chapter. Each section is labeled and includes activities that could be used within that chapter. The descriptions vary in detail as information pertaining to the activities is described during class. The activities are explained in general terms to enable them to be used by a variety of students and instructors. The activities may be crafted by each to make them unique. In addition, instructors may use the activities as graded or ungraded assignments. Although the use of the entire gamut of activities is up to the discretion of individual students and instructors, students are especially encouraged to read all of them to broaden and deepen their knowledge and understanding of the textbook and public speaking.

CHAPTER 1

Introduction to Public Speaking

Activities

☐ *Interview and Introduce a Peer*
☐ *Introduce Yourself*
☐ *Speech Class Inventory Survey*
☐ *Define Communication*
☐ *Transactional Model of Communication*
☐ *Types of Communication*
☐ *Benefits of Effective Public Speaking Skills*
☐ *Three Pillars*
☐ *Ethical Considerations*

Activity Name:
Interview and Introduce a Peer

Description: Interviewing a peer and then introducing him or her to the class

Instructions: Interview a peer who you don't already know with the questions provided. Write your questions/answers below. Introduce your peer to the class. Information to obtain during your one-on-one interview:

Name

Class year (freshman, sophomore, junior, senior)

Major/minor (areas of interest)

Where are you from?

Favorite TV show and/or movie

Best memory from the summer or holiday break ("family friendly")

What is your experience with public speaking?

What is your level of anxiety with public speaking? (scale of 1 low to 10 high)

Goal or passion in life

Five questions *you* have for your peer

Activity Name:
Introduce Yourself

Description: Introducing yourself using the basic speaking format

Instructions: Follow the basic speaking format for speeches – use an introduction, body, and conclusion.

In the Introduction, gain attention, establish credibility, articulate listener relevance, state your thesis, and preview your main points (tell them what you are going to tell them)

In the Body, present the information that you previewed in the introduction (tell them)

In the Conclusion, summarize what you talked about in the speech and end with a strong closing statement (tell them what you told them)

You should use a typed outline that has key words you should not write out your entire speech

Activity Name:
Speech Class Inventory Survey

Description: Answering questions about your public speaking experience

Instructions: Answer the questions.

Name:

Major:

What kinds of speaking experiences have you had in your classes, jobs, community, extracurricular activities, organizations, etc.? What was the size of the audience for each? What topics did you discuss?

What other courses are you enrolled in this semester that require speeches/presentations?

What do you find easiest about creating and delivering a speech?

What do you find difficult about creating and delivering a speech?

Do you have *severe* stage fright, stuttering, or anything else that might make it difficult for you to speak in public situations?

What techniques do you use to manage your public speaking anxiety?

How familiar are you with creating PowerPoint and/or Prezi presentations?

What is your process for practicing your speech?

Identify *three* aspects of speech preparation and delivery that you want to improve during this course.

Activity Name:
Define Communication

Description: Drawing how communication works

Instructions: Although we have been communicating since the moment we were born, most people have not looked at how communication works. Create a drawing that shows how communication works (please do not be concerned with your drawing ability for this activity). For example: If an alien asked you to draw how human communication works so they could understand our planet, what would you draw?

Activity Name:
Transactional Model of Communication

Description: Drawing the Transactional Model of Communication

Instructions: Without using your textbook, draw the Transactional Model of Communication below.

Activity Name:
Types of Communication

Description: Defining different types of communication

Instructions: Define, explain, and provide an example for each of the types of communication listed below.

Intrapersonal

COMMUNICATION WITH ONE'S SELF - SELF VOICE

Impersonal

Interpersonal

COMMUNICATION BETWEEN TWO OR MORE PEOPLE, USUSALLY FACE TO FACE

Group

COMMUNICATION BETWEEN 3 TO TEN PEOPLE, USUALLY FACE TO FACE

Public

SPEAKING TWO FIVE OR MORE PEOPLE, USUALLY AT A DISTANCE

Mass

INVOLVES DISTRIBUTION THROUGH RADIO, TV, AND OTHER

Digital and Computer-Mediated

INVOLVE GAMUT OF INTERACTIVE ACTIVITIES THAT ENCOMPASS ALL ASPECTS OF INTERNET & TECHNOLOGY.

Activity Name:
Benefits of Effective Public Speaking Skills

Description: Brainstorming ways effective public speaking skills can be beneficial

Instructions: With a peer, discuss how developing effective public speaking skills can be beneficial in the following areas:

College Courses

INSTRUCTOR - HIGHER QUALITY LECTURES, BETTER PEFORMING STUDENTS

STUDENTS - BETTER QUESTIONS, MORE PEER ENGAGEMENT

Professional Careers

HIGHER QUALITY PRESENTATIONS AND EXPLAITIONS OF FACTS

MORE LIKELY TO BE PROMOTED

Personal life

BETTER COMMUNICATION WITH PARTNERS AND FAMILY

MORE OPEN COMMUNICATION CHANNELS

You should be ready to report your ideas to the class.

Activity Name:
Three Pillars

Description: Drawing the three pillars and listing the important aspects

Instructions: Draw the three pillars of effective public speaking. List the important aspects under each pillar.

STRATEGY

STRUCTURE
PLANS
TACTICS
SEQUENCING
ORDER

CONTENT
PERTINANCE
RELEVANCE

DELIVERY
EYE CONTACT
HAND GESTURES
CONNECTION W/ AUDIENCE

AUDIENCE
CENTERED

How do having a strategy and understanding your audience relate to these three pillars of effective speaking?

Activity Name:
Ethical Considerations

Description: Brainstorming ethical considerations when designing and delivering a speech

Instructions: Brainstorm a list of ethical considerations when designing and delivering a speech. The ethical considerations can be for your speech topic or for a topic in general. After you have a full list, consider the potential consequences for the public speaker and audience – the consequences for good ethical choices and the consequences for bad ethical choices.

DO YOU BELIEVE IN THE CONTENT OF THIS SPEECH?

HOW LIKELY ARE PEOPLE TO CHANGE THEIR OPINION TO MATCH YOURS?

WHAT ARE THE RAMIFICATONS IF PEOPLE DO THIS?

NOTES:

CHAPTER (2)

Building Confidence

Activities

☐ *Public Speaking Anxiety Self-Assessment*

☐ *Gauging Public Speaking Anxiety*

☐ *Public Speaking Anxiety Strategies*

☐ *Managing Public Speaking Anxiety*

☐ *Finding Resources and Public Speaking Anxiety Exploration*

☐ *Personal Strategies for Managing Public Speaking Anxiety*

Activity Name:
Public Speaking Anxiety Self-Assessment

Description: Assessing Public Speaking Anxiety

Instructions: Follow the steps below.

Step 1:

Locate a public speaking anxiety assessment with your web browser

Step 2:

Answer each question in the assessment and record your data

Step 3:

Print the results and turn in during class

Activity Name:
Gauging Public Speaking Anxiety

Description: Gauging public speaking anxiety

Instructions: First, circle your perceived level of public speaking anxiety (on the scale – 1 is low and 10 is high).

Level of Speech Anxiety (Scale: 1 to 10)

High ↑   8 – 10

          6 – 7

          (3 – 5)

Low | 1 – 2

Second, describe how your perceived level of public speaking anxiety affects you in the following three ways:

Physically

SWEATY PALMS

TALKING QUICKLY

BROKEN EYE CONTACT

Mentally

MENTAL ROAD BLOCKS

OHMMMM

Emotionally

GRADE POINT ?

Third, describe your feelings toward public speaking anxiety during the following three time periods:

Your feelings before you speak

Your feelings at the start of your speech

Your feelings during your speech

Activity Name:
Public Speaking Anxiety Strategies

Description: Brainstorming a list of strategies used to manage public speaking anxiety

Instructions: Describe the strategies you have used in the past to manage your public speaking anxiety. Next to each strategy, indicate how effective those strategies have been in managing your anxiety.

Strategies/Techniques	Not Effective	Effective	Very Effective

Activity Name:
Managing Public Speaking Anxiety

Description: Sharing strategies for managing public speaking anxiety with other students

Instructions: Get together with two other students in class and exchange information on how they have experienced speech anxiety and the techniques they have used to manage their anxiety. Write those strategies below.

Strategies/Techniques	Not Effective	Effective	Very Effective

Activity Name:
Finding Resources and Public Speaking Anxiety Exploration

Description: Handling public speaking anxiety

Instructions: This assignment requires you to use resources (library and the Internet) to find information that will be useful to you in effectively managing your speech anxiety. Information from the textbook and the instructor are great resources, and it is important to gather information from other sources to help you in your efforts. You are required to find an article on public speaking speech anxiety, summarize the article, and identify how the information in the article may or may not be helpful to you (and others) in this course.

Follow the steps below.

Step 1:
Use a library research database or the Internet to find an article (scholarly or popular) concerning public speaking anxiety. You may want to be creative in your use of key words to find an article on the subject (e.g., public speaking, speech anxiety, speech fear, techniques, factors). Sift through many resources available on this topic to find an aspect that you connect with and/or find valuable.

Step 2:
Read the article closely.

Step 3:
In a typed document (12-point font, single or double spaced), write one or two paragraphs summarizing the article (e.g., what the article is about, the main points, interesting aspects).

Step 4:

After summarizing the article (Step 3), write one to three paragraphs briefly describing the following:

a. Your level of speech anxiety based on your previous public speaking experiences (on a 1±10 scale with 10 being the highest)

b. How you react to speech anxiety (how your anxiety manifests itself psychologically, emotionally, and physically)

c. How you have tried to "manage" your speaking anxiety in the past

d. How you think the information in the article is relevant to you and how you may or may not use the information in the article to help you become an effective public speaker (relating the information to your self-assessment of speech anxiety as well as to Chapter 2).

Step 5:

At the end of your typed document, include the citation for the article (identifying the bibliographic information such as the author, article title, link to where you found the article). If you want to use APA or MLA format, use library resources on APA or MLA to determine the correct format or use one of the APA or MLA websites to help you with the format. The citation should include the author name, date of the article, title of the article, volume number (and may be issue number depending on the source), page numbers, and a retrieval statement showing when the article was retrieved and the location (web address).

Step 6:

Bring the completed assignment with you to class and be ready to share the information you learned with your peers.

Activity Name:
Personal Strategies for Managing Public Speaking Anxiety

Description: Reflecting upon materials and activities to produce personal strategies for managing public speaking anxiety – Your Strategies

Instructions: After reading the chapter, sharing with peers, and participating in the chapter discussion, list the strategies you plan to use to manage your speech anxiety when preparing and delivering your speeches in this class.

NOTES:

CHAPTER  3

Analyzing and Adapting to the Audience

Activities

☐ *Defining and Understanding Audience Analysis*

☐ *Audience Analysis of the Class for Informative Speech*

☐ *Speech Situation Analysis*

☐ *Audience Analysis for a Public Speaking Event*

☐ *Adapting to Audience*

Activity Name:
Defining and Understanding Audience Analysis

Description: Understanding audience analysis in a general way

Instructions: Use Chapter 3 to answer the questions below.

Define audience analysis.

Why is audience analysis an important aspect of public speaking?

Describe a specific example of how understanding something about your audience would impact your speech and/or delivery.

List and define four of the demographic characteristics used to understand an audience.

List and define two of the "subject-related audience data" that a speaker should obtain during their audience analysis.

List two methods a speaker can use to analyze their audience (obtain data about their audience).

Activity Name:
Audience Analysis of the Class for Informative Speech

Description: Analyzing your class for your informative speech

Instructions: Think about your informative speech topic, analyze your audience (your class of public speaking students) and answer the following questions.

What do you think are the demographic characteristics of your audience?

What do you think is the "subject-related audience data" of the audience?

Based on this information, why would your audience be interested in listening to your topic and how are you going to connect your topic to your audience?

List at least three questions that you would like to ask your audience in order to better relate your speech topic to them (to better connect the topic to their interests, background, level of prior knowledge, etc.)?

List at least three questions that you would like to answer about the setting.

Activity Name:
Speech Situation Analysis

Description: Gathering information about the public speaking situation

Instructions: Get together with a peer or two (no more than three). You have been asked to deliver a speech on "being a college student" at the city's Chamber of Commerce. You are excited about the opportunity. In preparation for the speech, you need to learn as much as you can about the opportunity.

Your task is to come up with your own set of questions that you would need to ask the Director of the Chamber of Commerce revolving around the following three areas:

The Audience

The Speech Itself

The Setting

Activity Name:
Audience Analysis of a Public Speaking Event

Description: Gathering information about demographic, psychological, and environmental aspects

Instructions: Work with group members to develop a list of questions you would ask a host of a public speaking event. The questions should include the following:

Demographic Aspects (age, gender, ethnic background)

Psychological Aspects (attitude, values, and beliefs)

Environmental Aspects (speaking inside or outside, size of room, need for microphone)

Question to Host	Hypothetical Answer from Host	Strategy to Adapt and Craft

Activity Name: Adapting to Audience

Description: Creating an audience profile

Instructions: Create a speaking situation and audience profile, either for an upcoming speech or for a hypothetical speech, by completing the following steps:

Form groups

Identify the topic

Create two audience profiles

    demographic information

    psychological information

    environmental information

Identify if it is an actuation speech or a dispositional speech for each profile

Analyze and adapt to the different audiences by completing the following steps:

trade profiles with another group

analyze and record how the speech should change for each profile you received from another group

report to the class

Activity developed by Megan N. Bell and Jacob D. Bell

CHAPTER 4

Types of Support Strategies and Kinds of Support Materials

Activities

☐ *Matching Types of Support Strategies*
☐ *Matching Kinds of Support Materials*
☐ *Oral Citations*
☐ *Outline Puzzle*

ANALOGIES COMPARE FAMILIAR W/ UNFAMILIAR

ANCEDOTE: ALWAYS PACK READER'S DIGEST INTO FIRST AID KITS

COMPARE & CONTRAST: SIMPLARITIES & DIFFERANCES

DEFINITIONS CATEGORIZE & ARTICULATE MEANING. A BINARY

    CONTEXTUAL - HOW A WORD IS USED IN SET/SETTING
    DICTIONARY - CATEGORIZES WORDS/PHRASES
    ETYMOLOGICAL - ROOT WORDS TRACING AND HISTORY
    EXEMPLAR - POSTER
    NEGATIVE - THE WHAT IS BY WHAT IS NOT

$$A \neq \bar{A} \qquad A + \bar{A} = 1 \qquad A \cdot \bar{A} = \emptyset$$

    STIPULATIVE - ORIENTS AND REQUIREMENTS FOR AUDIENCE

DESCRIPTIONS CREATE IMAGERY

EXAMPLES PROVIDE EXXPANSION

Activity Name:
Matching Types of Support Strategies

Description: Matching the type of support strategy with the definition

Instruction: Draw lines to match the type of support material with the definition

Match the following definitions with the Types of Support Strategies

Analogies	Compare things that are familiar with things that are unfamiliar, extending beyond terse descriptions
Anecdotes	Brief narratives or short stories about humorous or interesting incidents
Comparisons and Contrasts	Illuminate similarities and differences
Definitions	Statements that categorize and articulate the meaning of a term, phrase, or concept, what something is and what something is not
Descriptions	Statements about the physical or psychological qualities of something such as an animal, object, or person
Examples	Statements that offer an expanded instance
Explanations	Statements that may tell *what, how*, or *why*
Facts and Statistics	Statements or states of affairs that are indeed the case and numerical representations of data
Instances	Brief examples, cases in point
Narratives	Statements that articulate meaning through short stories
Quotations	Statements made by the speaker attributed to someone else
Testimony	Provided by another witness or authority

Answers:

Analogies: Compare things that are familiar with things that are unfamiliar, extending beyond terse descriptions

Anecdotes: Brief narratives or short stories about humorous or interesting incidents

Comparisons and Contrasts: Illuminate similarities and differences

Definitions: Statements that categorize and articulate the meaning of a term, phrase, or concept, what something is and what something is not

Descriptions: Statements about the physical or psychological qualities of something such as an animal, object, or person

Examples: Statements that offer an expanded instance

Explanations: Statements that may tell *what, how*, or *why*

Facts and Statistics: Statements or states of affairs that are indeed the case and numerical representations of data

Instances: Brief examples, cases in point

Narratives: Statements that articulate meaning through short stories

Quotations: Statements made by the speaker attributed to someone else

Testimony: Provided by another witness or authority

Activity Name:
Matching Kinds of Support Materials

Description: Matching the kind of support material with the definition

Instruction: Draw lines to match the kind of support material with the definition

Match the definitions with the terms

Books	⑤	Credible, paper or online, because of review process	
Government Documents	①	Written works that can have comprehensive and extended coverage of a topic	⑤
Internet Documents	②	Information from government, nation, state, or community perspectives	①
Journal Articles		Found in open areas as well as secure areas	②
Magazines and Newspapers	④	Question-and-answer exchanges	③
Research Interviews	③	Snapshots of information from people from a particular time and place	④
Surveys		Written works, paper or online, that provide timely information	

Activity Name:
Oral Citations

Description: Writing statements to use while citing a source

Instructions: Review the resources and write a statement that could be used when implementing an oral citation during a speech (as well as included in the text of a formal outline):

Article Example (Paper Resource)

Article: Divorce is on the Rise

Author: Jackie Smith

Date of Article: July 11, 2013

Publication: *Newsweek*

Information: The primary reasons for divorce are finances and communication.

Statement: JACKIE SMITH IN 2013 WROTE ... FOR NEWSWEEK MAGAZINE.

Online Example (Internet Resource)

Article: Speed Dating

Author: Marcia Baker

Retrieval Date: October 7, 2013

Website: Lifestyles

Information: Speed dating is a new trend of the decade in dating.

Statement: ___ ••• ̶t̶o̶ ̶t̶h̶e̶ ACCORDING TO   LIFESTYLES .   COM ___

Interview Example

Interview Information:

Interviewee: Dr. Jane Smith

Interviewee's Affiliation: Horticulture Program

Information: Interest in organic farming will continue to increase.

Statement: Dr Jane smith w/ DEPT HORTICULTURE PROGRAM

Book Example

Author: J. S. Gordon

Book: *Helping Survivors of Domestic Violence: The Effects of Counseling*

Information: Domestic violence is a significant reason for many emergency room visits.

J.S. GORDON's BOOK...

IF YOU READ "HELPING..." YOU KNOW THAT

Statement: _____

Activity Name:
Outline Puzzle

Description: Constructing an outline and citing research

Instructions: Follow the sequence below.

View a video of an informative speech

Outline the informative speech

Cut the outline into individual components

Organize into pairs

Mix up the components of your cut-up outline

Reassemble the outline using the components (put the components in the correct sequence)

Review the video example of the informative speech that corresponds to the outline

NOTES:

Delivery

Activities

☐ *Types of Speech Delivery*

☐ *Effective and Ineffective Speaking*

☐ *Elements of Effective Delivery*

☐ *Filler Words*

☐ *Video Example*

Activity Name:
Types of Speech Delivery

Description: Defining and explaining different speech types

Instructions: Describe each of the following four speech types and provide an example for each (when it would be used).

Impromptu

Scripted (Manuscript)

Memorized

Extemporaneous

Activity Name:
Effective and Ineffective Speaking

Description: Considering qualities of effective and ineffective speaking

Instructions: Answer the questions below from your perspective as an audience member.

What qualities do you want to see in an effective public speaker?

What do effective public speakers do?

Which of your own characteristics help you (as an audience member) to understand the information and to stay connected to the speech?

What qualities do you NOT like to see in a speaker (what is annoying, distracting, makes you "tune out," etc.)

What do ineffective public speakers do?

If a speaker is ineffective, what impact does he/she have on you as an audience member?

Activity Name:
Elements of Effective Delivery

Description: Practicing your speech

Instructions: Address the statements below about practicing your speech.

Describe techniques you have used in the past to practice your speeches (when you practice, methods you have used, etc)

Indicate how effective those strategies were in preparing you for your speech

Next, get together with one or two other students in class and exchange information about techniques used. Write down each strategy. Evaluate each strategy for effectiveness

After writing down and evaluating each strategy, as well as after reading the chapter, sharing with peers, and participating in the chapter discussion: List the techniques you plan to use in practicing your speech

Activity Name:
Filler Words

Description: Eliminating filler words such as "um" and "ah"

Instructions: Follow the sequence below.

Get into groups of three or four

Deliver a one-minute impromptu speech on the topic provided by the instructor

Who can make it the longest without saying a "filler" word (um, ah)?

Goal: 60 seconds

Each student will be timed by another member of the group

As soon as a speaker says a filler word, the speech ends. Record the speaker's name and time in the area below

0, 10 seconds

11, 30 seconds

31, 50 seconds

51, 59 seconds

60 seconds!

Activity Name:
Video Example

Description: Evaluating speaker delivery

Instructions: Watch a video example of an Informative Speech and evaluate the speaker's delivery, addressing the aspects below.

Vocal Expressiveness

Movement in the Speaking Area

Hand Gestures

Eye Contact

Use of Note Cards

Use of Presentation Aid

Facial Expressions

Energy

Enthusiasm

Other

NOTES:

Presentation Aids

Activities

- ☐ *Bad PowerPoint Slideshow*
- ☐ *Bad Presentation Aids*
- ☐ *Bad PowerPoint Presentation*
- ☐ *Presentation Aids and Objects*
- ☐ *Observing PowerPoint Presentations*

Activity Name:
Bad PowerPoint Slideshow

Description: Exemplifying bad PowerPoint slides

Instructions: Follow the sequence below.

Construct a PowerPoint slideshow with multiple errors, write down all the errors in a list on the last slide

In the spirit of an expository informative speech, present information to your class about presentation aids while using your very badly constructed PowerPoint slideshow

Review all the errors with your classmates when you get to the last slide

Activity Name:
Bad Presentation Aids

Description: Creating examples of bad presentation aids

Instructions: Follow the sequence below.

Get into groups of two to develop a list of bad presentation aid ideas.

Once you and your partner complete your list, exchange your ideas with another group of two.

After you have reviewed all the ideas, merge as a group of four to discuss your ideas further.

Activity Name:
Bad PowerPoint Presentation

Description: Creating a terrible PowerPoint presentation

Instructions: Follow the sequence below.

In a group, generate a list of characteristics that make a PowerPoint difficult to view, feel free to magnify the characteristics

Incorporate the list of characteristics into a PowerPoint

As a group, present the PowerPoint to the class

Please note that the characteristics must be family friendly, do not include rude, discriminatory, or offensive material

Activity Name:
Presentation Aids and Objects

Description: Reinforcing a message with objects

Instructions: Follow the sequence below.

Determine your topic and message, perhaps create a theme such as "My Hometown" or "My Hobby"

Choose three objects to use during a speech, objects to help reinforce your message

Conceal the objects some way, in your pocket, in your coat, or under a cloth

Reveal the objects one by one and talk about each to tell your story and reinforce your message

Activity Name:
Observing PowerPoint Presentations

Description: Observing and critiquing PowerPoint presentations

Instructions: Study a PowerPoint presentation and answer the questions below.

Do the colors work, what is good and what is not good?

Does the design work?

Is the text suitable?

Do the graphics and clip art items reinforce the message?

Do the font or letter sizes work, what is good and what is not so good?

Do the transitions and other effects work, what is good and what is not so good?

Is the use of bullets functional and consistent?

Are background issues and foreground issues and contrasts at play?

Is there an appropriate amount of "stuff" on the slides?

Are there distractions?

Are there spelling errors?

Is wording uniform, such as capitalization?

Is wording parallel in structure when appropriate?

Is "blank slide" needed or used, if so, what is good and what is not so good?

CHAPTER 7

Introductions and Conclusions

Activities

☐ *Components of the Introduction*

☐ *Components of the Conclusion*

Activity Name:
Components of the Introduction

Description: Writing statements for each of the components of the introduction

Instructions: Follow the sequence below.

Review the chapter that contains information about introductions. Think about your topic for the informative speech. For each component of the introduction, write a statement for what you could say during your speech.

Attention Statement:

Listener Relevance Statement:

Speaker Credibility Statement:

Thesis Statement:

Main Point Preview Statement:

Watch a video example of an informative speech and identify each of the components of the introduction. For each component of the introduction, write a statement for what you heard.

Attention Statement:

Listener Relevance Statement:

Speaker Credibility Statement:

Thesis Statement:

Main Point Preview Statement:

Activity Name:
Components of the Conclusion

Description: Writing statements for each of the components of the conclusion

Instructions: Follow the sequence below.

Review the chapter that contains information about conclusions. Think about your topic for the informative speech. For each component of the conclusion, write a statement for what you could say during your speech.

Thesis Restatement:

Main Point Summary:

Clincher Statement:

Watch a video example of an informative speech and identify each of the components of the conclusion. For each component of the conclusion, write a statement for what you heard.

Thesis Restatement:

Main Point Summary:

Clincher Statement:

CHAPTER  8

Informative Speeches

Activities

- ☐ *An Expository Moment*
- ☐ *Selecting a Topic through Personal Inventory*
- ☐ *Selecting a Topic through Concept Mapping*
- ☐ *Selecting a Topic through Clustering*
- ☐ *Selecting a Topic through Questioning*
- ☐ *Informative Speech Outline Template – Inserting Strategies and Statements*
- ☐ *Informative Speech Formal Outline*
- ☐ *Revise Your Informative Speech*
- ☐ *Peer Critique of an Informative Speech*
- ☐ *Informative Speech Self-Analysis*
- ☐ *Informative Speech Self-Appraisal*

Activity Name:
An Expository Moment

Description: Teaching your audience a concept from the class

Instructions: Follow the sequence below.

Choose a public speaking topic from the textbook such as attention gaining statements, support materials, figures of speech.

Study the topic to become an expert to teach the audience the concept.

In the space below, list your topic, provide a definition of your topic, and provide an example of your topic.

Topic:

Definition:

Example:

When called upon to do so, present your topic to the class by listing your concept, defining your concept, and providing an example of your concept.

Activity Name:
Selecting a Topic through Personal Inventory

Description: Generating a topic for the informative speech

Instructions: Follow the sequence below.

Think about all the things in which you are interested, you have experienced. or you are involved in studying within your major.

Write those items of interest below these are potential topics.

Activity Name:
Selecting a Topic through Concept Mapping

Description: Generating a topic for the informative speech

Instructions: Follow the sequence below.

Select a preferred topic as an umbrella concept from your personal inventory.

Write that umbrella concept at the center of the page.

Think of potential sub-topics for that umbrella concept write them down.

Activity Name:
Selecting a Topic through Clustering

Description: Selecting topics and narrowing down a topic

Instructions: Follow the steps below.

Step 1
Generate a list of topics

Step 2
Create an idea web/cluster for one topic and then for another

    use the idea web/cluster to narrow your topic from something general to more specific

    identify your main points for your speech

Step 3
Choose at least two narrowed topics from the clustering activity, and complete Steps 4, 7 for each topic you are considering

Step 4
Consider your audience

Will they know anything about your topic?

How can you make it interesting to your audience?

What is unique about your topic or approach?

Step 5
Consider yourself the speaker

Are you familiar with the topic?

Are you comfortable speaking about the topic?

Are you an expert on the topic?

Do you want to speak about this topic?

Step 6
List potential ways you could gain attention

Step 7
List your potential main points for your speech body

Step 8
What is your narrowed informative speech topic?

Activity Name:
Selecting a Topic through Questioning

Description: Answering questions to help decide upon an informative speech topic

Instructions: Answer the questions below to help you decide upon your informative speech topic. Refer to pertinent areas of your textbook to help you answer the questions.

What is the general topic of your informative speech?
(*Example: Yellowstone National Park*)

What is the specific purpose of your speech (specific enough to be accomplished within the time requirements of the speech)?
(*Example: During the speech, I will inform the audience on three great places to visit in Yellowstone National Park.*)

Why did you choose this topic for your speech?
(*Example: I know a lot about Yellowstone because I've worked in the park and have visited the park many times. I have a lot of information regarding the park both personally and in books and on the Internet.*)

What are the two to four main points of your speech?
(*Example: The three main points of my speech are:*

Lake Hotel
Old Faithful
Mammoth Hot Springs)

List *three specific* "outside sources" that you may want to incorporate into your speech and *briefly describe* the reason(s) why you think each source would be helpful for you in developing your speech (from interviews, scholarly articles, Internet, book, etc.).
(*One Example of the Three Required Sources*)

The Wyoming Tourism website has great information about Yellowstone National Park that I could incorporate into my speech. The site includes information such as maps, history, location-specific information.

Why do you think your audience would be interested in your speech? How are you going to make your topic relevant to the audience (connect with them)?

(Example: I think the audience will enjoy learning about the world's first national park and the three places that are popular tourist areas. This information may be helpful if they are planning to visit the park one day. I will mention how many college students like to do outside activities, that many have been on vacation to great places such as national parks, and that there are opportunities to work in Yellowstone during the summer)

Activity Name:
Informative Speech Outline Template – Inserting Strategies and Statements

Description: Inserting the strategies for your informative speech by name along with the descriptive statement reflecting the strategy

Instructions: As you construct your informative speech, or after you have constructed your informative speech, insert the strategy by name for each area of your outline. For example the word "simile" is a strategy listed by name, and the descriptive statement "she is like a rose" is a descriptive statement that reflects that listed strategy. "Startling Statement" is another strategy listed by name for the attention category, and "Taxes will rise by 75% in the next two years" is a descriptive statement that reflects that listed strategy. In other words, list all the strategies and their descriptive statements in the outline template below.

Name: _____

Topic: _____

Purpose: _____

Introduction

Attention:

Name of Strategy _____

Descriptive Statement _____

Listener Relevance Cues:

Name of Strategy _____

Descriptive Statement _____

Speaker Credibility Statement:

Name of Strategy _____

Descriptive Statement _____

Thesis: _____

Preview Statement: _____

Body Name of Method of Organization _____

I. Main Point _____

   A. Name of Strategy _____

     Descriptive Statement _____

     _____

   B. Name of Strategy _____

     Descriptive Statement _____

     _____

II. Main Point _____

   A. Name of Strategy _____

     Descriptive Statement _____

     _____

   B. Name of Strategy _____

     Descriptive Statement _____

     _____

III. Main Point _____

   A. Name of Strategy _____

     Descriptive Statement _____

     _____

B. Name of Strategy _____

    Descriptive Statement _____

    _____

Conclusion

    Restatement of Thesis: _____

    Summary: _____

    Closing Phrase: _____

References

List references in APA or MLA format.

_____

_____

_____

_____

_____

_____

_____

_____

_____

_____

_____

_____

_____

_____

_____

_____

Activity Name:
Informative Speech Formal Outline

Description: Preparing a rough draft of your formal outline

Instructions: Use Chapter 8 (Informative Speeches) in your textbook to help you complete this outline draft.

This formal outline must have complete sentences, must have outline sequencing (numbers and letters, NOT bullet points), and must have outside research (kinds of support material) within the text of the outline and cited in the reference section.

The formal outline must have the following components:

Introduction (Five Components)

    Attention Gaining Statement

    Speaker Credibility Statement

    Listener Relevance Statement

    Thesis Statement*

    Main Point Preview Statement*

*Please note the thesis statement and main point preview statement can be combined.

Body

    Main Points (two to four main points are recommended)

    Sub-Points, one or two for each main point (that support each main point)

    Transition Statements (transitioning from one main point to the next)

    Support Strategies (Types and Kinds; orally cite sources during your speech)

Conclusion (Three Components)

    Thesis Restatement*

    Main Point Summary*

    Clincher Statement

*Please note that the thesis restatement and main point summary statement can be combined.

Reference Section

List the research you will cite during your speech list in APA or MLA format.

During your speech, you are required to orally cite at least two outside sources of research. For the research you cite during your speech, you must include citation information for that research within the reference section of your formal outline. A minimum of two reference sources must be included at the end of your formal outline (in APA or MLA style). Use online resources using a search engine to help you create your APA or MLA style citations.

Activity Name:
Revise Your Informative Speech

Description: Changing your audience and changing your plan

Instructions: Use your speech outline and your textbook to discuss the following aspects involved with revising your informative speech.

Identify a new audience, occasion, and time limit for your informative speech topic.

Describe characteristics of this audience (demographic, psychological, possible disposition toward topic/purpose, Chapter 3).

Describe how your speech purpose and your thesis would change for this new audience. If no change, explain why the original would be good for the new situation.

Describe examples of how you would use three of the support strategies discussed on pp. 24, 26 of the textbook.

Describe how (techniques from the book, Chapter 7) you would introduce the speech to the new audience with the goal of connecting the topic to them and motivating them to listen.

Describe how (again, techniques from the book, Chapter 7) you would conclude with the goal of making it motivating and memorable.

Activity Name:
Peer Critique of an Informative Speech

Description: Evaluating other speakers

Instructions: Receive direction from your instructor about which informative speaker to evaluate. Use what you have learned in class to evaluate that speaker (during his or her informative speech).

Use the speech components listed below to evaluate the speech. Make sure to include both your name and the name of your peer (who you are evaluating). This critique will be given to the student so make sure your comments are helpful and professional. To complete this activity, complete Sections 1 and 2 below.

Section 1: Analyze the micro- and macrostructure of the speech (speech components).

As you watch the speech, pay close attention to the items in the introduction, body, and conclusion; and then answer the five questions in the "Questions to Answer" part of this section.

I.   Introduction

    Attention Gaining

    Speaker Credibility

    Listener Relevance

    Thesis Statement

    Main Point Preview

II. Body (what were the main points?)

    Main Points (clear)

    Main Points Organized Appropriately

    Transitional Statements (clear)

    Two Outside Sources Kinds of Support Material (Research) Orally Cited

III. Conclusion

    Thesis Restatement

    Main Point Review

    Clincher Statement

Questions to address in your peer speaker evaluation:

Did the speaker include each of the items above and were they effective?

Identify components/items that were missing from the speech

Provide feedback regarding components/items that could have been better/stronger/more effective (in your opinion)

As an audience member, was the "structure/organization" easy to follow?

As an audience member, was the "content" helpful in understanding the speech topic?

Section 2: Analyze the speaker's delivery

As you watch the speech, pay close attention to the items pertaining to the speaker's delivery.

Delivery Components:

For items 1, 5 below, write short comments regarding each of the following aspects of the speaker's delivery (in your paper).

Appearance/Posture/Confidence

Eye Contact (with the entire audience for 90% of the speech time)

Body Movement (not stuck in one spot, use of helpful gestures, etc.)

Voice Expressiveness (not monotone; clear, good volume, etc.)

Facial expressiveness (face, eyes, smile, etc.)

Questions to address:

After watching the student's speech and commenting on items 1, 5 above, answer each of the questions below based on your perceptions of the speaker's delivery.

What did the student do well with his/her delivery?

Was there anything distracting with the student's delivery that reduced the effectiveness of the speech?

How could the student's delivery be made more effective?

Activity Name:
Informative Speech Self-Analysis

Description: Reflecting upon your own speech, critiquing yourself

Instructions: Critique yourself using three important components of public speaking: *content, organization,* and *delivery.* Answer the questions below in a paragraph-formatted typed paper, 12-point font, double spaced – minimum of three full pages, maximum of five. You should include a title page with information such as your name, section number, assignment, and date.

You need to provide evidence and examples in your paper. In answering the questions, your paper should be written in a narrative format (fully developed paragraphs with at least three sentences per paragraph not in a question and answer format).

The following questions may help guide your self-reflection. You don't have to answer each question listed but they do provide you with an idea of the kinds of items to reflect upon during your self-analysis (and in writing this paper).

Questions to Address in Self-Analysis Paper:

Why did you choose the topic you did?

Did you include all of the five components of the introduction in your speech?

Was the information you provided in your introduction effective? What would you do differently to make your introduction more effective?

Do you think your introduction attracted the attention of the audience? How do you know? What "listener relevance link" did you use to connect your audience with your topic?

What speech pattern did you use to organize the body of your speech?

Did you use effective transitions after your main points 1 and 2?

Did the body of your speech seem "balanced" (the same amount of information and time was devoted to each main point)?

From an audience standpoint, do you think your speech was organized effectively and appropriately? Why or why not?

Did you include all of the three components of the conclusion in your speech?

Was the information you provided in your conclusion effective?

After watching the video and reflecting on your speech, what would you do differently in your conclusion to make it more effective?

What impact do you think your message had on your listeners?

What nonverbal feedback cues did you get from the audience while you were delivering your speech?

How did that feedback affect you?

How dynamic do you think your delivery was during this speech? How could it have been improved?

Did you maintain eye contact with at least 90% of the audience?

Did you make eye contact with the entire audience?

Did you do anything that you think the audience might have found "distracting?"

How appropriate was your rate of speech?

How appropriate was your volume?

How appropriate was your pitch/tone?

How appropriate was your use of body movement?

Did you think you looked or sounded nervous?

If your speech was recorded, what would you do differently in delivering your speech to make it more effective?

Were you anxious before and during the speech?

How did you manage your anxiety before and during your speech?

How much time did you invest in practicing your speech?

How did you practice (and did this method work for you)?

Overall, what were your main strengths in your speech?

Overall, what were your main weaknesses in your speech?

What do you wish you had done/said that you did not do/say?

What three things (be specific) will you try to improve in future speeches that you may deliver (for school or job)?

Activity Name:
Informative Speech Self-Appraisal

Description: Assessing your speaking

Instructions: Follow the sequence below.

Reflect upon your speech

Address each category of the instructor assigned evaluation form in written form

NOTES:

Persuasive Speeches

Activities

- ☐ *Stranded on a Raft*
- ☐ *Persuasive Speech Topic*
- ☐ *Determining Logos, Pathos, and Ethos*
- ☐ *Identifying Personal Credibility*
- ☐ *Persuasive Speech Outline Template – Inserting Strategies and Statements*
- ☐ *Post Persuasive Speech Evaluation*
- ☐ *Post Persuasive Speech Self-Appraisal*

Activity Name:
Stranded on a Raft

Description: Speaking to survive on a raft – reflecting logos, pathos, and ethos

Instructions: Receive the following instructions from your instructor.

You need to understand that a ship has sunk and you are a survivor on a raft in the middle of the ocean (you are situated with other students in three chairs in front of the classroom)

One by one, you verbalize to the class why you should be able to stay on the raft, and perhaps why one of the other two should be bumped into the ocean. Central to the activity, one student is bumped into the ocean after each speaking round (a speaking round is complete after each student has spoken, with counterpoints)

After the round, your "fate" as a survivor will be determined by the ocean "gods" (the ocean gods are the remaining students in the class – the students in the class vote who should stay and who should be bumped. Your fellow students can vote an unlimited number of times. One of you is bumped after each round until there is a winner.)

If you receive the most votes, you win the persuasive speaking contest.

After you conclude this activity, you need to reflect upon how your words and the words of your fellow students connect to logos, pathos, and ethos.

Activity Name:
Persuasive Speech Topic

Description: Getting organized – determining your topic, position, and support

Instructions: Record your answers to the questions below. Use the same practices used to select and narrow your Informative Speech topic to help you determine your Persuasive Speech topic (personal inventory, research, concept mapping, clustering).

What is the topic for your persuasive speech?

Why do you think your audience will be interested in your topic (why should they care)?

What is your position on this topic (your claim)?

What are the main points of your speech (to help support your argument/claim)?

What organizational structure (argument structure) are you going to use to structure your information and persuade the audience?

List three specific "outside research sources" that you may want to incorporate into your speech (author, article/resource title, link). For each of these three items, describe the reason(s) why you think each source would be helpful for you in developing your speech (from interviews, scholarly articles, the Internet, books). Please note that listing "library" or "government site" is too general and, therefore, will not be accepted for this assignment. In other words, you need to be specific.

List two questions that you would like to ask the audience to help understand them better as well as their position on your argument.

Activity Name:
Determining Logos, Pathos, and Ethos

Description: Watching a video of a persuasive speech to determine the logos, pathos, and ethos

Instructions: Follow the sequence below.

Watch a video

Identify the logos (sense of logic), pathos (feeling of emotion), and ethos (aura of credibility). Write down the findings.

Activity Name:
Identifying Personal Credibility

Description: Exploring your areas of credibility

Instructions: Answer the questions below.

Think of something you are legitimately knowledgeable about (academics, trivia, athletics, hobbies)

Write down three to four statements to explain why you have more knowledge about that topic than an average person

Write down one example to support/clarify each of the statements

Select two statements, with their examples, and deliver this short speech to an audience

Activity Name:
Persuasive Speech Outline Template – Inserting Strategies and Statements

Description: Inserting the strategies for your persuasive speech by name along with the descriptive statement reflecting the strategy

Instructions: As you construct your persuasive speech, or after you have constructed your persuasive speech, insert the strategy by name for each area of your outline. For example, the word "simile" is a strategy listed by name, and the descriptive statement "she is like a rose" is a descriptive statement that reflects that listed strategy. "Startling Statement" is another strategy listed by name for the attention category, and "Taxes will rise by 75% in the next two years" is a descriptive statement that reflects that listed strategy. In other words, list all the strategies and their descriptive statements in the outline template below.

Name: _____

Topic: _____

Purpose: _____

Audience: _____

Introduction

Attention:

Name of Strategy _____

Descriptive Statement _____

Listener Relevance Cues:

Name of Strategy _____

Descriptive Statement _____

Speaker Credibility Statement:

Name of Strategy _____

Descriptive Statement _____

Statements to Set the Context:

Name of Strategy _____

Descriptive Statement _____

Thesis:_____

Preview Statement: _____

Characters Body – Name of Method of Organization _____

I. Main Point_____

  A. Name of Strategy _____

    Descriptive Statement _____

    _____

  B. Name of Strategy _____

    Descriptive Statement _____

    _____

II. Main Point_____

  A. Name of Strategy _____

    Descriptive Statement _____

    _____

B. Name of Strategy _____

    Descriptive Statement _____

III. Main Point _____

    A. Name of Strategy _____

       Descriptive Statement _____

       _____

    B. Name of Strategy _____

       Descriptive Statement _____

       _____

Conclusion

Restatement of Thesis: _____

Summary: _____

Action: _____

Closing Phrase: _____

References

List references on a separate page in APA or MLA format

_____

_____

_____

_____

_____

_____

_____

_____

_____

_____

Activity Name:
Post Persuasive Speech Evaluation

Description: Reflecting upon your speaking

Instructions: In a typed document, answer the questions below.

Compared with the informative speech, how did *your* delivery go with the persuasive speech (what did you do to improve, what went better, what went worse, what aspects of your delivery are still "working against you," etc.)?

For the persuasive speech, beyond delivery, what worked well and what would you have changed if you had to do it over again (e.g., content, organization, information, research, citing research, persuasive wording)?

How will you use your experiences delivering the persuasive speech to improve on the speeches you will make in the future (for other class and/or in the job)?

Activity Name:
Post Persuasive Speech Self-Appraisal

Description: Assessing your speaking

Instructions: Write a paper

Reflect upon your speech

Address each category of the instructor assigned evaluation form in written form

NOTES:

CHAPTER 10

Special Occasion Speeches

Activities

☐ *Modus Operandi*

☐ *Special Occasion Speech Outline Template – Inserting Strategies and Statements*

☐ *Adapting Speech Planning to Special Occasion Contexts*

☐ *Video Examples of Special Occasion Speeches*

☐ *Speech of Tribute*

Activity Name:
Modus Operandi

Description: Using an underlying form for special occasion speeches

Instructions: Create statements for each aspect of the modus operandi. Note that the statements do not have to be in a sequence. The statements can be integrated creatively.

Consider your special occasion speech topic? Write it down

Set the criteria for what would be really "good" or "great"? Write it down

Fulfill the criteria with examples of how the person achieves the standards? Write it down

Connect the ideas to the audience? Write it down

Activity Name:
Special Occasion Speech Outline Template – Inserting Strategies and Statements

Description: Inserting the strategies for your special occasion speech by name along with the descriptive statement reflecting the strategy

Instructions: As you construct your special occasion speech, or after you have constructed your special occasion speech, insert the strategy by name for each area of your outline. For example, the word "metaphor" is a strategy listed by name, and the descriptive statement "she is a rose" is a descriptive statement that reflects that listed strategy. In special occasion speeches, the modus operandi involves the following: state a criterion, fulfill the criterion with examples, and make a connection with the audience. For example, a special occasion speech could be about the top student in the class. To set a criterion, you might say "Top students attend every class," "Top students receive the highest grades," and "Top students participate in class discussions." To fulfill this criterion, you might choose a specific student by name and list examples of him or her fulfilling the criterion. Finally, to make a connection with the audience, you might indicate how the audience can do a better job in those three areas. In regard to the references at the end, let's say you are giving a special occasion speech about your favorite sports person and find statistics in a book, the Internet, or elsewhere. You need to reference any source you use in a reference page as well as verbally in your speech.

Name: _____

Topic: _____

Purpose: _____

Audience: _____

Introduction

Attention:

Name of Strategy _____

Descriptive statement _____

Listener Relevance Cues:

Name of Strategy _____

Descriptive Statement _____

Speaker Credibility Statement:

Name of Strategy _____

Descriptive Statement _____

Statements to Set the Context:

Name of Strategy _____

Descriptive Statement _____

Thesis: _____

Preview Statement: _____

Body Name of Method of Organization _____

I. Main Point _____

   A. Name of Strategy _____

     Descriptive Statement _____

     _____

   B. Name of Strategy _____

     Descriptive Statement _____

     _____

II. Main Point _____

    A. Name of Strategy _____

       Descriptive Statement _____

       _____

    B. Name of Strategy _____

       Descriptive Statement _____

       _____

III. Main Point _____

    A. Name of Strategy _____

       Descriptive Statement _____

       _____

    B. Name of Strategy _____

       Descriptive Statement _____

       _____

Conclusion

Restatement of Thesis: _____

Summary: _____

Action: _____

Closing Phrase: _____

References

List references on a separate page in APA or MLA format

_____

_____

_____

_____

Activity Name:
Adapting Speech Planning to Special Occasion Contexts

Description: Writing and revising the speech to adapt to a different audience and context

Instructions: Identify a special occasion that could include speeches

Describe the occasion

Describe the attendees

What makes it special?

Develop a speech of welcome to that occasion

Identify and describe an award that might be presented at such an occasion

Activity Name:
Video Examples of Special Occasion Speeches

Description: Watching video examples of special occasion speeches and critique

Instructions: Find three video examples (may find online examples), write the title of the videos, and under each title write your thoughts. Discern the modus operandi as discussed in the textbook.

Activity Name: Speech of Tribute

Description: Constructing a Speech of Tribute

Instructions: Create a 2–3 minute speech that recognizes and celebrates accomplishments. It may center on people, groups, or events.

Accomplishments and events are usually celebrated for two basic reasons. First, they are important themselves, and second, they are important as symbols. When you plan a speech of tribute, consider both the actual and the symbolic values that are represented. Speeches of tribute are a time for warmth, pride, and appreciation. Your manner should reflect these qualities as you present the tribute.

Use the following two techniques: identification and magnification.

> Identification create associations and close feelings among the members of the audience and between the audience and the speaker. Promote identification through the use of narratives, the recognition of heroes, or a renewal of group commitment.

> Magnification select certain features and dwell on them. Magnify them until they fill the minds of listeners and characterize the subject. Emphasize values and establish themes. Point out how the person has overcome great obstacles, how the person has accomplished something unusual, or how the person has produced a superior performance. Point out that the person had pure motives, not selfish, and that the accomplishment has benefited society.

> Language tools use metaphor and similes to magnify the subject through creative associations. Compare and contrast to make selected features stand out; dramatize certain events as stories that unfold over time; or use causation to present selected features as the powerful causes of certain effects. Build the speech to a crescendo until it concludes.

Guidelines:

Do not exaggerate the tribute so that it becomes unbelievable

Focus on the honoree rather than yourself

Create vivid, concrete images of accomplishments

Tell stories that make those accomplishments come to life

Be sincere

NOTES:

ADDENDUM

Activities

- ☐ *Take Aways – Reflection*
- ☐ *Peer Evaluation Form*
- ☐ *Assess a Peer's Speech*
- ☐ *Evaluate a Proficient Speaker*
- ☐ *Post Speech Self-Evaluation*
- ☐ *End of Semester Self-Evaluation*

Activity Name:
Take Aways – Reflection

Description: Reflecting upon the class

Instructions: Follow the sequence below.

Reflect upon what you have learned in the class

Choose an item that really sticks out in your mind that was interesting and helpful

Choose an item that really sticks out in your mind that you need to improve upon in future speaking opportunities

Activity Name:
Peer Evaluation Form

Description: Evaluating a peer

Instructions: Evaluate a peer using the form below.

Name: _____

Speaker's Name: _____

Speech Title/Topic: _____

1. Could you identify the attention strategy and was it effective? Why?

2. Was the thesis statement clear and accurate? Did the body of the speech fulfill your expectations based on the thesis/preview statement? Explain.

3. Did a clincher statement in the conclusion provide a strong sense that the speech was about to end? If not, how could it have been improved?

4. What were three strengths of the speech/speaker?

5. What are two things the speaker can work to improve the next speech?

6. Additional comments:

Activity Name:
Assess a Peer's Speech

Description: Assessing a peer's speech

Instructions: Follow the sequence below.

During student speeches, assess a fellow student's speech

Indicate three areas of strength

Indicate three areas of weakness

Provide three statements about how the student can improve

Assess a Peer

Assess a Peer

Assess a Peer

Assess a Peer

Assess a Peer

Assess a Peer

Assess a Peer

Assess a Peer

Assess a Peer

Assess a Peer

Assess a Peer

Assess a Peer

Assess a Peer

Assess a Peer

Assess a Peer

Activity Name:
Evaluate a Proficient Speaker

Description: Evaluating a speaker other than a student or an instructor

Instructions: Pay close attention to a speaker other than a student or an instructor (e.g., College 101 Workshops, Diversity Awareness Events, International Study Abroad Programs, Mayor of the City Speeches, President of the Kiwanis Club Speeches, workshops, guest speeches). Carefully watch the efforts and answer the following questions in a *typed* document.

Please note:

The speaker you evaluate *cannot* be a student or instructor.

The speaker you observe and evaluate must deliver his or her speech during the semester (you cannot evaluate a speaker who delivered the speech before the beginning of the semester).

The completed document must be turned in to the instructor within two weeks after the date the speaker was evaluated.

Format:

In a typed document (double or single spaced), include the following information at the top of the first page.

Your name

Speaker's name

Name of the event

Topic of the presentation

Date of the presentation

Time of the presentation

Location of the event

In addition, answer the following questions. You can use a "question/answer" or narrative paragraph format to answer the questions. If you use the "question/answer" format, you need to include the question (fully typed out) and the answer to the question.

Questions to answer

Did the speaker organize the speech in a way that was easy to follow and understand?

Did the speech have a clear introduction, body, and conclusion? If you answered "no" to any of these questions, please explain.

What kind of supporting material did the speaker use (e.g., examples, definitions, narratives, testimonies, statistics, orally cited research)?

Did the speaker start and end on time? If you answered "no," please explain.

Describe elements of the speaker's delivery that made the speech effective (e.g., movement, hand gestures, eye contact, vocal delivery)?

Describe elements of the speaker's delivery that distracted you from his or her message (if there were any)?

Do you think the speaker understood the audience (may have conducted an "audience analysis" before the speech)? Explain why you think the speaker did or did not understand the audience.

How did the speaker connect the topic with the audience?

What were your overall thoughts regarding the public speaker?

Activity Name:
Post Speech Self-Evaluation

Description: Analyzing your own speaking

Instructions: Reflect upon your speaking using the form below.

Name: _____ Speech Title/Topic: _____

Preparation

Reflect on the preparation process. What steps did you take to prepare your speech?

What part(s) of the preparation process worked well?

What part of the preparation process needs improvement? What are three things you will do to improve the preparation process for your next speech?

Delivery

What were three of the strengths of your speech delivery?

What were three weaknesses of your speech delivery? What are three things you will do to improve these weaknesses for your next speech?

Activity Name:
End of Semester Self-Evaluation

Description: Assessing the development of your public speaking skills

Instructions: Consider items such as a self-assessment exercise during the first week of the semester in which you identified strengths, weaknesses, and areas to work on during the course and/or your public speaking anxiety test. Use this information as a starting point.

In essay form, discuss how you developed your public speaking skills. Include comments about *all* of the following:

Areas in which you now feel confident, as both speech writer and speech presenter

Specific strategies or techniques you feel comfortable using as a speech writer and as a presenter

Examples of what and how you learned about public speaking from listening to other speakers in class

Areas for improvement you perceive now that you have a larger perspective on the whole process of speech making

A plan for how you will continue to develop your speech making skills and confidence in the wider world outside this learning laboratory

NOTES: